PTSD RECOVERY

Practical Mind-body Tools to Heal Trauma

(For Trauma Recovery and Healing to Regain Control of Your Mind)

Louis Denault

Published by Tomas Edwards

© **Louis Denault**

All Rights Reserved

Ptsd Recovery: Practical Mind-body Tools to Heal Trauma (For Trauma Recovery and Healing to Regain Control of Your Mind)

ISBN 978-1-990268-52-6

All rights reserved. No part of this guide may be reproduced in any form without permission in writing from the publisher except in the case of brief quotations embodied in critical articles or reviews.

Legal & Disclaimer

The information contained in this book is not designed to replace or take the place of any form of medicine or professional medical advice. The information in this book has been provided for educational and entertainment purposes only.

The information contained in this book has been compiled from sources deemed reliable, and it is accurate to the best of the Author's knowledge; however, the Author cannot guarantee its accuracy and validity and cannot be held liable for any errors or omissions. Changes are periodically made to this book. You must consult your doctor or get professional medical advice before using any of the suggested remedies, techniques, or information in this book.

Upon using the information contained in this book, you agree to hold harmless the Author from and against any damages, costs, and expenses, including any legal fees potentially resulting from the application of any of the information provided by this guide. This disclaimer applies to any damages or injury caused by the use and application, whether directly or indirectly, of any advice or information presented, whether for breach of contract, tort, negligence, personal injury, criminal intent, or under any other cause of action.

You agree to accept all risks of using the information presented inside this book. You need to consult a professional medical practitioner in order to ensure you are both able and healthy enough to participate in this program.

Table of Contents

INTRODUCTION 1

CHAPTER 1 NECESSARY CONDITIONS BEFORE STARTING WORK 14

CHAPTER 2: I REALLY WANT TO MAKE HIM HAPPY. THINGS ARE SO PLEASANT WHEN HE IS. WHY DO I FEEL SO FRUSTRATED AND LIKE A FAILURE IF HE IS NOT HAPPY? . 21

CHAPTER 3: PMDS THE SYNDROME THAT CAUSES PTSD. 26

CHAPTER 4: GET A DOG 33

CHAPTER 5: NEUROLOGICAL EXPRESSION OF PTSD 37

CHAPTER 6: NEUROLOGICAL EXPRESSION OF PTSD 50

CHAPTER 7: THE QUEST TO TREAT PTSD BETTER 54

CHAPTER 8: APPOINTMENT PREPARATION 88

CHAPTER 9: EMOTIONAL AND PHYSICAL TRAUMA – METHODS OF OVERCOMING THEM 97

CHAPTER 10: MIND BODY SYNERGY 113

CONCLUSION 121

Introduction

As Larson's quote above embodies, some of us are innocently thrust into lives, a family, personal relationships, romantic partnerships, or school or career situations that often feel more like a brutal boxing match, a ravaging roller coaster ride, or a volcano of toxic activity, rather than a nurturing upbringing, a healthy home life, a professional network, a supportive career or educational setting, or a pleasant, mutually respectful friendship. Do any of these descriptions sound a bit too familiar to you right now as you struggle with complex PTSD?

How many of you presently live with the poisonous plagues or perilous pitfalls of complex PTSD? Are you still shrinking in the shadows of shame and sin from childhood or adolescent traumas? Have you experienced physical, psychological, emotional, and/or sexual abuse and terror over the course of your lifetime or within the past several years (or even decades)? Has the loss of a loved one catapulted you into the complex claws of PTSD, a precarious path without a mindful map or any concrete escape plan as it involves numerous intersections, roadblocks, and pot holes on our minds, bodies, and spirits daily?

Unlike treating a broken bone with a cast, the path to healing from complex PTSD is one that can take dangerous detours and boisterous bumps on the road to recovery and resilience (literally!). Tan's quote about wounds is so valid and applicable to the visible and invisible ones that impacted my body, mind, and soul. Are you even conscious of your wounds from complex PTSD? Did you endure or witness atrocious acts of domestic violence or intense scenes of intimate partner violence (IPV) when dating, married, or while growing up in a dysfunctional household or volatile situation? Are you currently still harboring woes and wounds beyond words from service in the military, exposure to war and violence as a former refugee or immigrant, or endured atrocious acts of rape, molestation, incest, or sexual assault? This book will offer you some light amid the darkness that you have had to deal with for far too long.

Were you ever a victim from a natural disaster, school violence, mass shooting, political plot, racial profiling, or hate crime? Have you developed PTSD after living in poverty, engaging or viewing gang violence, witnessing domestic or vivacious street crimes, or been bullied or cyberbullied to the point of complex PTSD? In turn, this book offers a nonjudgmental approach to first recognize and then holistically heal and repair those seething scars on our minds, hearts, bodies, and souls. I will then equip you with empowering ways to achieve vital knowledge, relevant research, practical tips, and daily applications to better address, cope, regain, and heal your life from complex PSTD more naturally and holistically in this flexible workbook that is all about you and your needs.

Specifically, the overall objective of this workbook is to give you the teachable tools, renewed confidence, resources, and motivations to rebound with resilience and mindfulness from complex PTSD. My use of a Dracula quote may seem to be a bit odd or goth, but the notions of "hope and enjoyment" resonate with my goals as a writer here. Thus, you are so more than a label, notes in a chart, comment on a therapist's couch, or damaged goods from the past! Thus, this book is rooted in the empowering notion that you can define yourself without succumbing to the shackles and chains that inflict furtive flashbacks and perpetual pains from complex PTSD.

While this book will not automatically cure or totally erase entire chapters of complex PTSD from your life or memory, it will definitely guide you toward greater acceptance, mindful release, personal enlightenment, and inner peace. I will share my own personal stories from 45 years of living with family members with PTSD from military service in WWII and the Vietnam War, coupled with intergenerational poverty, and endless cycles of violence and domestic abuse.

Despite having two postsecondary degrees and escaping my own dire circumstances from my childhood and adolescent years of turmoil, rural poverty, dating violence, and witnessing domestic abuse, I was still eventually diagnosed in my 30s with complex PTSD after living under the daily dysfunction, crazy chaos, and undeniable unpredictability that characterized my upbringing until my 20s. Although I thought I was immune to PTSD since I accrued these higher educational degrees that combined many psychological courses and research, achieved world travel to over 50 countries to study their indigenous ways of healing, and worked abroad in Asia for many years, the pinnacle of mindful living, I could not escape the powerful PTSD pit. I fell even further into the PTSD abyss after my first marriage at a young, immature age to an abusive partner, schemer, and master manipulator.

My complex PTSD also took root in my career. Just as Lorde expresses, PTSD does not take a single route or manifest in a "single-issue" in our lives. I then chose professional work that spanned over 15 intense years in a field with at risk, homeless, urban teens, who were often victims of gang violence, America's foster care system, bullying, domestic and sexual abuse, homelessness, substance abuse, poverty, and racial discrimination, and more complex PTSD exposure. However, I can proudly attest that I am now finally free of PTSD's power plays over my mind, body, relationships, voice, choices, career, finances, and spiritualty. What can I offer you in this book that others on the market in the same niche may not be able to provide? For starters, I passionately devote this book to paying it forward and sharing some of the keys to emancipation that freed me from complex PTSD on professional, spiritual, psychological, sexual, socioemotional, financial, behavioral, physical, and personal levels.

In essence, I adamantly encourage you to live, learn, and love beyond the PTSD label. If I did it, despite a life story that sounds more like a Lifetime movie channel special than one's autobiography, then what is stopping you today? Although you might have acquired the PTSD diagnosis or live with it in an undiagnosed form or imminent predisposition, there is true hope and help knocking at your door. This workbook delivers easy, affordable, personalized, and successful ways to heal yourself and rise above the grief, hopelessness, triggers, pain, anger, depression, and anxiety that complex

PTSD has pummeled you with presently. Are you ready to live happily, healthily, holistically, and much more mindfully without the guilt, anger, sadness, and anguish from labels today?

As we work together in this workbook to rip off the lame labels, maimed memories, and stinging stigmas that can force us to live under a guise of grief and despair from complex PTSD, you will be able to achieve the following objectives (and more) after reading this book:

Define PTSD in your own words, without all the medical jargon.

Understand what complex PTSD is and trace its common sources

Articulate your past traumas via the Word Up I and II Ice Breakers

Integrate the power of words as transformative and healing via the Started from the Bottom Exercise

Recognize the overlapping ramifications from complex PTSD as far as physical, cognitive, psychological, spiritual, socioemotional, sexual, behavioral, financial, and vocational challenges

Recall how complex PTSD impacts your holistic health and happiness using the Spring-Cleaning Exercise

Set attainable, personalized, realistic goals using the Why Me? Exercise

Complete the Be Kind to Rewind Exercise to develop better self-awareness about your own complex PTSD's causes and sources

Modify your health problems into "wealth" pride using the Health to Wealth Strategy

Discuss various PTSD treatments that are holistic and mindful in nature

Reflect on how the Say Yes: Treatment Talk exercise can deliver holistic healing and professional support in your coping mechanisms.

Learn ways to integrate the Silence Your Inner Critic application

Embrace the healing power of exercise and movement to cope with complex PTSD

Brainstorm and then apply some ABCS of Movement to your life

Generate 3 AHA Moments to synthesize new learning from the workbook

Obtain tips for regulating relationships, improving communications, and enriching social skills

Acquire the 2-Step Prep activity for emotional healing

Employ more boundary work to regulate healthy relationships in your life

Formulate a Music of the Heart playlist to increase emotional regulation

Learn more emotional regulation and management techniques to exude confidence, balance, health, happiness, and resilience, despite complex PTSD

Plan to add more self-care into your daily life and routines

Find a safety symbol to guide your emotional regulation and healing efforts

Realize the impact on your own sexuality from complex PTSD

Discuss the role of power plays in healing from sexual traumas

Devise your own POWER Acrostic Reflection

Discover ways to leap over lies from sexual abuse in your past

Transition from a "mind full" to mindful approach to heal from PTSD

Live in the present moment, free from pain, shame, and memories of complex PTSD

Apply more positive psychological premises and tactics to your own life and coping mechanisms

Practice formulating and articulating I-Statements for more emotional regulation

Acquire specific workplace tips to succeed against complex PTSD for career, leadership, professional, and economic stability

Add the WHOMP, There It Is Activity to your workplace toolboxes and techniques to manage PTSD proactively.

Apply more Hocus Focus words and techniques to calm yourself and center

Benefit from the Break Dance technique to enhance your goal setting acquire chunking techniques to incorporate for work and school successes

Discover the merits of self-talk to heal from your complex PTSD

Practice using Talking the Talk tactics.

Understand why and how self-advocacy can ensure better productivity at work and school

Recognize 8 Great Work Woes and strive to address them proactively and mindfully

Identify safe words to enable you to gain resilience in your recovery process.

Gain a plethora of resilience strategies to survive and thrive amid complex PTSD

Perform the AHA Finale to plan and celebrate all your meaningful and successful healing work from this book.

Chapter 1 Necessary Conditions Before Starting Work

It's essential to comprehend your working environment rights and obligations with respect to pay and conditions, wellbeing and security and working environment harassing.

By law, your boss is answerable for ensuring:

your workplace is sheltered and giving suitable defensive hardware if important

laborers are free from segregation and tormenting you get every one of your qualifications as far as pay and conditions.

As a specialist, you are answerable for:

Understanding the states of your work. This incorporates knowing your pace of pay, working hours and privileges to breaks and leave working in a way that isn't unsafe to the wellbeing and security of yourself or others comprehending what to do in the event that you think your boss isn't meeting their duties.

Ensure you:

Comprehend the states of your business. This incorporates your pace of pay, working hours and your qualifications for breaks, leave and open occasions realize your privileges concerning segregation and harassing. Realize what to do in the event that you experience or witness this in your working environment know the wellbeing and security necessities of your work environment. Ability to keep up a protected situation for yourself as well as other people approach the entirety of the fitting wellbeing apparatus and gear. Recognize what to do in case of a mishap realize where to find support on working environment wellbeing and security issues pertinent to your state or domain.

Consistently I get notification from individuals urgently attempting to become fruitful business visionaries. They unavoidably have heaps of essential inquiries that right away reveal to me they've dove in rashly and, subsequently, have seriously restricted their odds of making it all alone.

I'm certain that is not what you need to hear, however on the off chance that I don't come clean with you, at that point who will? The issue is that is the incorrect method to do it. The hands-down most ideal approach to turn into an effective business visionary is to do whatever it takes not to turn into a business visionary in any case.

Pause, what? That doesn't bode well. It seems like a logical inconsistency.

On the contrary, it makes total sense. Not just that, it's the best counsel on business you'll ever get. The thing is, no one turns into a fruitful business visionary as time goes on by embarking to get one. It happens naturally under specific conditions.

Related: 10 Behaviors of High Achievers

The issue is one of aggressive markets. Enterprise is about business, and a business that beats the challenge and takes off isn't so natural to create. For a dare to have even barely any possibility at all of making it, a few variables need to meet up:

Opportunity.

Like it or not, openings don't simply fly out of your Mac's screen and yell, "Here I am!" You need to go out and discover them and investigate them. Consider openings branches off a tree trunk. You have to get out in the genuine working world to pick up presentation to enough branches. That is the place everything else originates from.

Disclosure.

Maybe the hardest thing about a business is making sense of the correct client issue that should be illuminated. Without that, you have nothing. As a rule, that requires critical introduction, skill, and experience. Else, you'll never think of a triumphant item that beats the challenge.

Ability.

Each fruitful business visionary has a type of skill when they think of the item or organization that winds up making it. Possibly it was their obsession from the very first moment or maybe they created it while working for other people. Whichever it is, there's something they can show improvement over the pack … and BSing isn't it.

Related: Quit Screwing Around and Get to Work System.

Regardless of whether its value accomplices with the correct blend of ability, financial specialists, grown-up supervision, or some mix thereof, effective organizations quite often have a few key players required from the beginning or generally at an early stage. That requires a system – not an online one, a genuine system of genuine individuals you meet in reality.

Sagacious.

Not to be buzzword, yet organizations have heaps of moving parts and it is difficult to get everything cooperating except if you have a type of business insightful. There are just three spots to discover that: from your family, from business guides, or by working hands-on in the business world.

Notice that the variables cover. They're in reality all interwoven. That is the reason not embarking to turn into a business person however getting out on the planet and getting your hands grimy working is the least demanding approach to some time or another make it all alone. The genuine business world is the place each one of those conditions meet up. Furthermore, that is the place best business visionaries discover them. The main admonition is that I accept that you're searching for a type of breakout achievement where that turns into your vocation and you bring home the bacon at it. Obviously, you can slug it out with a gazillion rivals in various private companies or find success with it as a solopreneur, yet that is not actually taking the ball out of the recreation center, if you catch my drift. See, I realize this may be frustrating for some of you, however trust me when I let you know, on the off chance that you truly need to become showbiz royalty sometime in the future, you'll be ideally serviced by getting out and getting some understanding than slamming your head against a divider attempting to make sense of why things aren't working out for you.

Chapter 2: I Really Want To Make Him Happy. Things Are So Pleasant When He Is. Why Do I Feel So Frustrated And Like A Failure If He Is Not Happy?

Where in the world did we get that mandate inside of us that we are responsible for making others happy? And why does it take most of our lives to figure out that not only do we not **have to**, we **can't**. It is not our job to keep anyone happy. Not our husband, our children, our boss, our friends, our coworkers, our parents, the mailman, strangers, or anyone. Even if it were our responsibility to keep everyone happy, it is not humanly possible. And in my experience, even God does not make it His aim to keep everyone happy. There must be something even better. Higher. More important than a temporary feeling.

But in the meantime, while we are living day to day with other people, it truly is nicer when we are all happy. And most of us would sacrifice in order to keep that pleasantness in our homes. The problem is that when we spend all of our good energy on an impossible task, we end up spent. Depleted. And ultimately no one is happy.

Felicia was on the verge of a major meltdown. How did she get to that point without realizing there was a problem? Like many of us, Felicia really loved her vet, Trent, and did all she could to show it. However, somewhere along the way, she forgot her own needs. In her case, due to a health issue, she was limited in spare energy for social occasions.

Sometimes as well meaning as he was, Trent would forget about her limitations and make plans for them without discussing it with her. This particular occasion was a late evening out for dinner and a show with friends. When he informed her of the plans, she wanted to implode. She panicked inside! At that moment, she saw two options: Either say okay and keep him happy at the expense of her health and pay for it all the next week, or say no for her health and risk his anger, which would backfire and make her lose more energy ultimately from the conflict.

The following is an excerpt from her journal as she worked through the dilemma:

"I am feeling tempted to abandon myself and my needs to keep him happy. Part of me is trying to be determined not to go because I know what it will do to me. I am afraid that I will crash and take a real setback, which I dread especially because I have been doing so much better lately. It really bothers me that he did not talk about it with me first. Ticks me off! We need to get better at deciding things together. Well, I will plan to stick up for myself graciously, but it feels very uncomfortable. Scary. But I promised my body I would start listening to it more and not subjecting it to suffering to keep others happy.

"I told him that I was sorry I could not join them tomorrow. Trent is not happy. At all. But I am taking care of myself and he is not happy about my boundaries. It is scary, but something inside me feels stronger. I know it is right, but doing this is new to me. Why do I feel I have to fight for it? But if I gave in I would be sicker. I would be so resentful, and they would not necessarily be any happier as a result.

"Felicia, be strong; be gracious. Love myself and nurture me and don't be afraid that they may not like it. Help me God to do the right thing and do it graciously.

"And what a free feeling to remember that he does not have to be happy all the time. How freeing!"

Felicia and Trent had a really good talk after all had settled down. She was able to share her needs and articulate them better. And he was able to talk about his perspective too. They are doing much better. And Felicia has been meltdown-free for a good while now.

Another loved one of a veteran with PTSD adopted this phrase somewhere along the way on her journey. She no longer feels obligated to run herself into the ground attempting to keep everyone happy. Most of us would also benefit from adopting it as our own. Her phrase is, "It's my turn!"

All the work we put in to trying to keep them happy can be more useful if we invest it in keeping ourselves healthy. Working hard to keep from setting them off will only distance us from them and burn us out. But when we focus on being ourselves and living life fully, then we are more fulfilled and the relationship can grow. And the more we are good to us, the better it is for them.

Chapter 3: Pmds The Syndrome That Causes Ptsd.

Now the thing that help created PTSD especially in soldiers, is called PMDS. It stands for Paranoia, Mission list, Devalued Syndrome. Let me explain, When we were in the military we were trained to always be on the lookout (high alert) for the enemy. We were taught how to identify a potential threat or enemy. Weather it was Charile,(Vietnam) the Iraqi, the Taliban or Isis etc.

Paranoia: We were program to always be in a paranoid state of mind, because our life and the lives of others were at risk. In the military we always had guard duty, even if there was no war or threat, keeping us in a tense paranoid condition. We were never taught how not to be paranoid once we were no long in the service. Therefore PARANOID tense state of mind is now a part of who we are.

Most ex military soldiers don't even realize this. But now that you do you can talk yourself out of this by being more aware of the fact that you are no longer in that kind of intense danger.

Mission less: When we were in the service we felt important. We were told and we felt that we had a purpose/mission. We felt deep down inside that we were better than the average person on the streets because, we had and we knew what our purpose in life was. Everyone wants to know what their purpose/mission in life is right?

But once we left the service, for whatever reason, we no longer had a mission a purpose. We didn't feel important any more, therefore we felt MISSION LESS!

Devalued: Out here in the real world (civilian world) we often feel disrespected and dishonored. The average person has no Idea the type of intense leadership training, life survival training, and under pressure decision making skills we have been taught.

We go and get a job (paying less than what we are really worth, but at least it's a job right) and start working for a supervisor who has no leadership skills, half your age, with no experience in life, and shows you no respect for who you are(a veteran),what you know, or what you have been through, and is defiantly less qualified at being a leader than you are. You feel disrespected depressed, and DEVALUED!

Clearing your mind
Those who take up any subject with an open mind, willing to learn anything that will contribute to their advancement, comfort, and happiness are wise. The law of clearing states that within every challenge and period of your life, what is the source of all solutions and opportunities is made available and visible to you. You will need to go through a process of clearing out old beliefs and

opinions in order to make yourself ready to take full advantage of the power of the new solutions and opportunities of the universal law.

A large component of learning something new is to be open to hearing it. Sometimes that requires pushing past your current ideas of what makes sense, and keeping your mind open to new ideas and possibilities. Not everything can be explained in a way that seems logical.

Some of the most groundbreaking discoveries of our time came about because the inventor was brave enough to tackle a subject with a new way of thinking about it. It's time to let go of resistance, doubt and fear which will keep you stagnant to embracing new things.

It will also be difficult for you to share anything new with the world and enjoy new experiments or discoveries. It's OK to question things and debate a subject. However, when you are truly interested in communicating, learning, and can do so without any preconceived idea about the outcome of the conversation, you accept new thoughts and then process and explore them with an open mind and heart. This takes practice. Just because we don't believe something doesn't make it untrue.

When it comes to universal law, it's no question, it is law. If you do not believe in gravity for example, does that mean it doesn't exist? Of course not. Gravity exists even if you don't believe it does. Now of course because you do believe it does you see evidence of it every day. And that's true of all universal laws, they are in existence every day, every moment, whether you believe in them or not. Now let's look at the key points of this law.

Key point number one:
1. Having an open mind will allow you to learn more, advance quickly, and experience more joy in your life.
Key point number two:

2. Having an open mind may mean looking past things that seem contradictory and operating on faith.

Key point number three:

3. Allow messages and their meaning to come to you in their own time. If you force something it pushes it further from you. You will learn what you need to learn in the time that it is right for you to learn it.

Key point number four:

4. Resistance, especially in accepting new ideas, keeps us closed off and unable to fully experience new things and experiences.

Key point number five:

5. By clearing out your mind and your life of those things that have taken up space but provided little value, you make room for more meaningful things to take their place.

Now let's talk about how you apply this law by eliminating the mental clutter. Often times mental clutter is made up of worries, negative thoughts, past experiences, doubt, and a million little things that don't serve us. This mental clutter can overshadow the present. The easiest way to clear mental clutter is by processing the thoughts rather than letting them take over your brain.

Chapter 4: Get A Dog

There are four major programs that pair a patient with PTSD with either a Labrador or a golden retriever. The idea was launched in 2008 by a social worker named Rick Yount and the concept is for the dog to spent 4 to 6 weeks with the patient.

Animals can make even the most isolated personality come out and become emotional. This helps patients with PTSD, overcome the emotional part of the disorder which is the denial of what happened. Teaching the dog to do various things improves the communication skills of the patient which in turn improves the denial of conversation and dealing with what happened.

Another very helpful aspect of the assistance a dog offers, is the ability of its owner to relax enough to be able to get some sleep, as the owner now knows that they do not have to worry about their safety as someone else has undertaken this task.

Some hidden properties of bonding with a dog is that such a connection increases the production of oxytocin which is a hormone that is directly correlated to trust and the ability to perceive and interpret facial expressions. This reduces the paranoia that comes with PTSD during the social intercourses.

So far 300 people has been studied after the time they spent with a dog and the results were staggeringly positive. This research made the PTSD service dogs as one of the major alternative treatment options that do not need psychotherapy and medications.

If you participate in a program of PTSD service dogs you will be given a dog that has been trained. But this is not really necessary. The key that a dog is a good PTSD treatment, is that it offers companionship without criticism and friendship that is always there. You will not have to go look for it anywhere.

Dogs appeal to your emotions. You do not have to train a dog to do that. They do it naturally. Labradors and golden retrievers have been selected as most suitable for being what is called emotional support dogs, as, for some inexplicable reason, they display the best understanding of the problem their owner faces. Of course, it doesn't have to be one of the two. Any dog will do.

For those who hate dogs it is very difficult to achieve the same result with other animals. Cats are too independent for training. A dolphin would be an even better option than a dog but you cannot have it as a pet at home. If you cannot have a dog, you may try to find another kind of animal that will share your problem with you and never leave your side.

A bonus to getting a dog that is not in a program is that you will not have to give it back to the program after six weeks. You get to keep it for life.

Chapter 5: Neurological Expression Of Ptsd

Three areas of the brain in which function may be altered in PTSD have been identified: the prefrontal cortex, amygdala, and hippocampus. See the diagram of the brain below:

Regions of the brain associated with stress and posttraumatic stress disorder.

A prospective study using the Vietnam Head Injury Study showed that damage to the prefrontal cortex may actually be protective against later development of PTSD. In a study by Gurvits et al., combat veterans of the Vietnam War with PTSD showed a 20% reduction in the volume of their hippocampus compared with veterans having suffered no such symptoms. This finding could not be replicated in chronic PTSD patients traumatized at an air show plane crash in 1988 (Ramstein, Germany).

In human studies, the amygdala has been shown to be strongly involved in the formation of emotional memories, especially fear-related memories. Neuroimaging studies in humans have revealed both morphological and functional aspects of PTSD. **However, during high stress times the hippocampus, which is associated with the ability to place memories in the correct context of space and time, and with the ability to recall the memory is suppressed.** This suppression is hypothesized to be the cause of the **flashbacks** that often plague PTSD patients. When someone with PTSD undergoes stimuli similar to the traumatic event, the body perceives the event as occurring again **because the memory was never properly recorded in the patient's memory.** The previous diagram does not show the location of the hippocampus, but the diagram below clearly indicates this vital neural component. The diagram shows the **ventral** part of the brain:

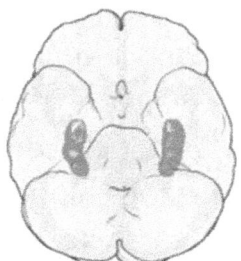

The areas in red represents the hippocampus

The hippocampus is a small, curved formation in the brain that plays an important role in the limbic system. The hippocampus is involved in the formation of new memories and is also associated with learning and emotions.

Because of brain symmetry, the hippocampus is found in both hemispheres of the brain on the ventral surface. When both sides of the hippocampus are damaged, the ability to create new memories can be impeded. If damage is restricted to just one side of the brain, memory function will remain nearly normal.

Age can also have a major impact on the functioning of the hippocampus. By the time an adult reaches 80 years of age, they **might** lose as much as 20 percent of the nerve connections in the hippocampus. Those who experience such loss show significant declines in memory performance.

Who Gets PTSD?

Many people face life threatening, even terrifying events during their lifetime, but do not develop PTSD. So who get PTSD? Many soldiers during wartimes face identical conditions in which their life is in jeopardy, but not all of those soldiers develop PTSD. Why the discrepancy in the expression of this condition?

Many studies have been conducted to try and answer the above questions. Most of the conclusions reached by investigators point to one unifying fact, and that is

those who been a witness to violence, or have been a victim of violence have a stronger predisposition to the development of PTSD later in life, when once again placed in a terrifying situation

Family Violence

Trauma from family violence can predispose an individual to PTSD. However, being exposed to a traumatic experience does not automatically indicate someone will develop PTSD. It has been shown that intrusive memories, such as flashbacks, nightmares, and the memories themselves are greater contributors to the biological and psychological dimensions of PTSD than the event itself. These intrusive memories are mainly characterized by sensory episodes, rather than thoughts.

People with PTSD have intrusive re-experiences of traumatic events that lack awareness of context and time. These episodes aggravate and maintain PTSD symptoms, since the individual re-experiences trauma as if it were happening in the present moment.

Clinical findings indicate that a failure to provide adequate treatment to children after they suffer a traumatic experience, depending on their vulnerability and the severity of the trauma are more susceptible to PTSD symptoms in adulthood.

Genetics

There is evidence that susceptibility to PTSD has a hereditary link. It has been approximated that as much as 30% of the expression of PTSD is caused from genetics alone:

* For twin pairs exposed to combat in Vietnam, having a monozygotic (identical) twin with PTSD was associated with an increased risk of the co-twin's having PTSD compared to twins that were dizygotic (non-identical twins).

* There is also evidence that those with a genetically smaller hippocampus are more likely to develop PTSD following a traumatic event.

* Research has also found that PTSD shares many genetic influences common to other psychiatric disorders. Panic and generalized anxiety disorders and PTSD share 60% of the same genetic variance.

* Gamma-aminobutyric acid (GABA) is the major inhibitory neurotransmitter in the brain. A recent study reported a genetic variation of GABA may predispose an individual to PTSD.

* PTSD is a psychiatric disorder that requires an environmental event that individuals may have varied responses to, so gene-environment studies tend to be the most indicative of their effect on the probability of PTSD than studies of the main effect of a particular gene.

Genome-wide association study (GWAS) offers an opportunity to identify novel risk variants for PTSD that will in turn inform our understanding of the etiology of the disorder. Early results indicate the feasibility and potential power of GWAS to identify biomarkers for anxiety-related behaviors that suggest a future of PTSD. These studies will lead to the discovery of novel loci for the susceptibility and symptomatology of anxiety disorders including PTSD.

Risk Factors

Most people (more than half) will experience at least one traumatizing event in their lifetime. Men are more likely to experience a traumatic event, but women are more likely to experience the kind of high impact traumatic event that can lead to PTSD, such as interpersonal violence and sexual assault. Only a minority of people who are traumatized will develop PTSD, but they are more likely to be women.

The average risk of developing PTSD after trauma is around 8% for men, while for women it is just over 20%. The risk is believed to be higher in young urban populations (24%): 13% for men and 30% for women. Rates of PTSD are higher in combat veterans than other men, with a rate estimated at up to 20% for veterans returning from Iraq and Afghanistan.

Posttraumatic stress reactions have not been studied as well in children and adolescents as adults. The rate of PTSD may be lower in children than adults, but in the absence of therapy, symptoms may continue for decades. One estimate suggests that the proportion of children and adolescents having PTSD in a non-war torn population in a developed country may be 1% compared to 1.5% to 3% of adults, and much lower below the age of 10 years.

Predictor models have consistently found that childhood trauma, chronic adversity, and familial stressors increase risk for

PTSD as well as risk for biological markers of risk for PTSD after a traumatic event in adulthood. Traumatic experiences in children is a predictive indicator of the development of PTSD later in life. This effect of childhood trauma, which is not well-understood, may be a marker for both traumatic experiences and attachment problems. Proximity to, duration of, and severity of the trauma also make an impact, and **interpersonal traumas** cause more problems than impersonal ones.

Quasi-experimental studies have demonstrated a relationship between intrusive thoughts and intentional control responses such that suppression increases the frequency of unwanted intrusive thoughts. These results suggest that suppression of intrusive thoughts may be important in the development and maintenance of PTSD.

Military Experience

Researchers Schnurr, Lunney, and Sengupta **identified risk factors** for the development of PTSD in Vietnam veterans. The subjects were 68 women and 414 men of whom 88 were white, 63 black, 80 Hispanic, 90 Native Hawaiian, and 93 Japanese American. Among their findings were:

Hispanic ethnicity, coming from an unstable family, being punished severely during childhood, childhood anti-social behavior, and depression as pre-military factors.

War-zone exposure, depression as military factors

Recent stressful life events, post-war trauma, and depression as post-military factors

They also identified certain **protective factors**, such as:

Japanese-American ethnicity, high school degree or college education, older age at entry to war, higher socioeconomic status, and a more positive paternal relationship as pre-military protective factors

Social support at homecoming and current social support as post-military factors. Other research also indicates the protective effects of social support in averting PTSD or facilitating recovery if it develops.

Researchers Glass and Jones found early intervention to be a critical preventive measure.

PTSD symptoms can follow any serious psychological trauma, such as exposure to combat, accidents, torture, disasters, criminal assault and exposure to atrocities or to the sequel of such extraordinary events. **Prisoners of war** exposed to harsh treatment are particularly prone to develop PTSD. In their acute presentation these symptoms, which include subsets of a large variety of affective, cognitive, perceptional, emotional and behavioral responses which are relatively normal responses to gross psychological trauma. If persistent, however, they develop a life of their own and may be maintained by inadvertent reinforcement. Early intervention and later avoidance of positive reinforcement (which may be subtle) for such symptoms is a critical preventive measure.

Studies have shown that those prepared for the potential of a traumatic experience are more prepared to deal with the stress of a traumatic experience and therefore less likely to develop PTSD.

Chapter 6: Neurological Expression Of Ptsd

Three areas of the brain in which function may be altered in PTSD have been identified: the prefrontal cortex, amygdala, and hippocampus. See the diagram of the brain below:

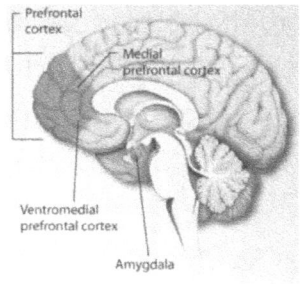

Regions of the brain associated with stress and posttraumatic stress disorder.

A prospective study using the Vietnam Head Injury Study showed that damage to the prefrontal cortex may actually be protective against later development of

PTSD. In a study by Gurvits et al., combat veterans of the Vietnam War with PTSD showed a 20% reduction in the volume of their hippocampus compared with veterans having suffered no such symptoms. This finding could not be replicated in chronic PTSD patients traumatized at an air show plane crash in 1988 (Ramstein, Germany).

In human studies, the amygdala has been shown to be strongly involved in the formation of emotional memories, especially fear-related memories. Neuroimaging studies in humans have revealed both morphological and functional aspects of PTSD. **However, during high stress times the hippocampus, which is associated with the ability to place memories in the correct context of space and time, and with the ability to recall the memory is suppressed.** This suppression is hypothesized to be the cause of the **flashbacks** that often plague PTSD patients. When someone with PTSD undergoes stimuli similar to the traumatic event, the body perceives the event as occurring again **because the memory was never properly recorded in the patient's memory.** The previous diagram does not show the location of the hippocampus, but the diagram below clearly indicates this vital neural component. The diagram shows the **ventral** part of the brain:

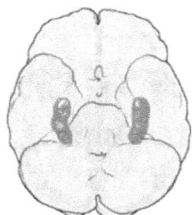

The areas in red represents the hippocampus

The hippocampus is a small, curved formation in the brain that plays an important role in the limbic system. The hippocampus is involved in the formation of new memories and is also associated with learning and emotions.

Because of brain symmetry, the hippocampus is found in both hemispheres of the brain on the ventral surface. When both sides of the hippocampus are damaged, the ability to create new memories can be impeded. If damage is restricted to just one side of the brain, memory function will remain nearly normal.

Age can also have a major impact on the functioning of the hippocampus. By the time an adult reaches 80 years of age, they **might** lose as much as 20 percent of the nerve connections in the hippocampus. Those who experience such loss show significant declines in memory performance.

Chapter 7: The Quest To Treat Ptsd Better

For many with post-traumatic stress disorder, relief is evasive. But research determining the source of signs is spurring new restorative approaches. It may even be possible to stop PTSD before it begins.

As a 21-year-old tank commander in the Israel Defense Forces, Yuval Neria saw comrades and close friends badly hurt and killed in the 1973 Yom Kippur War. He himself suffered serious injury when his tank was hit, but that didn't keep him from taking command of other tanks, for which he received the Medal of Valor, Israel's highest combat award. He served again in 1983.

His experience on the Sinai front in 1973 vividly informs Fire, a war novel he wrote that captures the terror, nerve, aggravation, and confusion of fight. It also decreed his life's work.

" The Yom Kippur War taught me a lot about the destructive effect of extreme combat," says Neria. "I comprehended fear very well, extreme fear, fear for your life," he says. "I knew a lot of people who ultimately developed PTSD; I felt really connected to them, I wanted to be included." He ended up being a scientific psychologist specializing in trauma, then a scientist probing its roots. In 2001, in the immediate wake of the World Trade Center attacks, New York's Columbia University recruited him to head its Research and Treatment Program for PTSD.

He saw it as "a chance to follow what I would felt was my destiny because of my experience in war." Neria never ever had post-traumatic stress disorder, but "what I carry with me, in addition to the horror and the fear of war, is a comprehension of what clients are going through and a commitment to their treatment."

War, of course, is not the only experience that stamps the brain so strongly that it remains constantly alert to threats, sees them where they might not exist, and gets memories of scared events so readily and vividly they overwhelm daily activities. Nor is it the sole catastrophe that shows up the emotional torture during the night, taunting sleep with the faces or weeps of kids, or partners, or comrades who could not be saved from harm.

Fires, hurricanes, plane crashes, automobile accidents, sex abuse-- any unexpected, violent interruption, even a life-threatening disease like cancer-- can leave a mark. And so Neria has carried out studies not only of veterans and prisoners of war and citizens under rocket attack but also of earthquake survivors, those who've endured sexual assault, people who lost loved ones on 9/11, and those straight exposed to the 9/11 attacks in New York City.

At Columbia, Neria is focused mostly on the neural mechanisms underlying PTSD. His work highlights areas of the brain associated with recognizing threats and keeping memories of afraid events. Neria and colleagues have determined abnormalities in how these areas look, how they work, and particularly how they fail to work together.

From his continuous studies, and those of many other scientists, efficient treatments are emerging. They target specific biochemical processes and brain circuits.

Not all of the treatments are new. Direct exposure treatment, for instance, has been around for decades, but combined with targeted natural treatments including particular drugs and delivered in novel ways, it promises relief for the nearly 50% of patients left by present methods, their whiplash reactivity driving them to withdraw from the world, or to navigate it with suspicion or anger, or to numb themselves with compounds that exchange one sort of real pain for another. There's also great new hope that there are ways to prevent PTSD from ever taking place.

Three Months, 3 Years-- or Forever

The existence of PTSD was formally acknowledged in 1980, when it was first included in psychiatry's Diagnostic and Statistical Handbook, then in its third edition. The condition, however, has been around very likely since the first hunter was whipped by a lion or the first temblor shook the earth.

PTSD is a reaction to experiencing or experiencing an event or series of events involving the risk of death or serious bodily damage. People with PTSD suffer from timeless anxiety signs, like insomnia and worry, and are often hypervigilant-- continuously alert to possible risks. They characteristically have an overstated startle response: Unforeseen noises, movements, or contact can provoke a strong, even violent response.

PTSD is defined by intrusive memories: The distressing event(s) is remembered spontaneously in flashbacks with the same panic, fear, and terror it originally evoked. Traumatic moods and ideas persist. They can take the form of anger, guilt, shame, or a feeling of detachment from others. Ideas like "Absolutely nothing good can happen to me" and "Nobody can be trusted" are common. To evade reminders of the trauma, patients may stay away from leaving the house.

The disorder "is not simply fear based," worries psychologist Paula Schnurr, executive director of the National Center for PTSD, a unit of the Veteran's Administration. It can show up as sadness-- complete with shame, guilt, and apathy-- or as anger and hostility.

The Inside Story of PTSD

When sensory areas of the brain discover a prospective danger, nerve impulses are instantly routed through the thalamus to the amygdala. Aroused, the amygdala generates the experience of fear and indicates the adrenal glands to produce adrenalin, raising heart rate and high blood pressure to set in motion the body for sudden action.

For more continual mobilization, the hypothalamic-pituitary turning point swings into equipment, tripping off a waterfall of body hormones culminating in the release of cortisol, which extends the mobilization reaction. It also keeps the amygdala activated, keeping the state of high alert. In such an aroused state, strong memories are readily formed, and they have staying power.

Under typical conditions, the thinking brain brakes amygdala activation, bringing mobilization to a halt when it concludes that threat is past, and the hippocampus puts the episode in the setting of past experience. With PTSD, people stay hypervigilant, on the lookout for danger even in everyday scenarios. Fear memories are easily awakened-- common sounds, sights, and even ideas trigger recollection of the terrible event so clearly that it feels just as if it is happening again.

Armand Cucciniello III was a diplomat at the United States Embassy in Baghdad throughout the Iraq War, living and operating in the Green Zone, a compound secured by tall concrete walls topped by barbed wire. "But rockets and mortars lobbed or fired overhead had no issue permeating it," recalls Cucciniello. Attacks began during the troop rise of spring 2007, 6 months after he showed up. "My first exposure was the worst: I heard a woman die just meters away."

There was no pattern to the attacks. "You never ever knew what would happen or when. After a year of off-and-on bombardment, I was extremely tense, highly emotional. I would well up just as though I wanted to cry, for no reason," Cucciniello recalls.

A psychiatrist told him he had PTSD and prescribed an antidepressant. The drug helped his emotional control, but even years later, "loud noises, doors slamming, anything like a boom would activate me. Time would stop for a few seconds, and I would be incapacitated," he says. On a check out to family in New York City, the dull thump of a taxi discussing an iron plate covering street building and construction-- not loud, but "the specific pitch of a rocket taking off"-- could provoke a flashback.

He had trouble sleeping for several years, and even now, if he tries going off his medication, "every little thing comes back-- the tense feeling, the welling up of tears." Cucciniello has happened with his life and is now an advisor to four-star Army General Robert Abrams, who heads the United Nations Command in South Korea.

There's been a great rise of interest in biological markers that identify the changes brought on by PTSD and that could be used to anticipate and diagnose the disorder, Schnurr reports. With brain-imaging tools like magnetic resonance imaging, scientists are getting a dynamic picture of the flashback memories, the fear, and other state of mind disturbances common of the disorder. The National Center now also preserves a brain bank, a repository of postmortem tissue samples from PTSD victims, to facilitate investigation into the molecular machinery giving life to the symptoms.

" We see at the very least three areas included," Neria reports. They include the amygdala, which regulates feeling and is ground zero for processing fear; the hippocampus, where memories are processed for storage and retrieval; and areas of the prefrontal cortex, the planning and choice center of the brain, which generally has the capacity to moisten amygdala activity.

In the wake of a traumatic event, he says, circuits of communication amongst the three regions are interrupted, accounting for the harmful vitality of traumatic memory. "In PTSD, the amygdala is hyperactivated and the prefrontal cortex and hippocampus are underengaged, leaving patients extremely restless and haunted by their distressing experiences, the memories appearing and reappearing involuntarily" with a strength unblemished by time.

" Attempting to acquire power over those memories and their associated anxiety, nightmares, and flashbacks, we see a lot of avoidance-- people stay away from talking about their trauma, attempting to manage their anxiety level," says Neria. They avoid situations that might trigger recollection. "Numbing of emotion comes later-- clients end up being more depressed than excited." Fifty percent of people with PTSD, in fact, also experience depression.

Neurobiologist Benjamin Suarez-Jimenez, a member of Neria's laboratory, employs virtual reality to explore the tendency to see threat where there is none. While in an MRI scanner, subjects video-walk through a meadow selecting flowers. In some areas, they are stung by bees-- represented by mild electric shocks. In others, they are not. "Healthy controls learn to distinguish between safe and hazardous areas, becoming hyperaroused only in areas where they were stung. Most people with PTSD overgeneralize; they don't discriminate accurately between safe and threatening parts," Suarez-Jimenez finds.

He is trying to pinpoint the brain parts accountable for the overgeneralization of danger. In earlier work, he identified the brain networks activated when healthy subjects make safe-dangerous differences, and is now collecting information on PTSD clients. "We want to compare brain activity, physiology, and self-ratings of anxiety in people who have never experienced extreme trauma, those who have and developed PTSD, and those who were resilient."

Although most brain-imaging work offers essential insights, some findings have direct scientific application. Some studies in his laboratory and in other places suggest that "the size of the hippocampus is an essential to response to treatment," says Neria. "We found that clients who have a bigger hippocampus develop less PTSD over time and do better." Tests revealing a small hippocampus may well indicate the need for medication and psychotherapy focused on reprocessing their memories.

Psycho-therapy contributed for Philip Robinson. "Being a survivor is rather challenging," says Robinson, who, 30 years ago last August, started the steamer Marchioness, in addition to 130 others, most in their 20s, to celebrate the birthday of a London good friend. He was beneath deck when a substantial barge riding high in the Thames essentially ran over the boat and sent it down in seconds. "I was struck in the shoulder and hit by flying bottles. I just swam and swam. I'm a professional vocalist, and I kept hold of my breath. I got out through a broken window." Fifty-one others didn't.

And Robinson did well till, 11 years after the catastrophe, a public query got underway. "We had to relive the accident. There were interviews, investigations. My relationship broke down. I was having trouble at work." A check out to his GP resulted in a full psychiatric assessment. "I was experiencing sadness. My typically robust coping systems had been challenged and overwhelmed." Two years of work with a therapist followed. He was motivated to let go of the belief that "I was singing for dead friends." He now sings for himself. "Singing is a manner in which my soul can speak with tragedy."

Because Robinson is the first to acknowledge how luckily the aspects of his life worked for him, he's set up a charity to help other victims of single-incident disasters get whatever help they're found to really need. Every year his charity, the Antonio Vasconellos Fund, gives out 51 grants-- each in the name of a Marchioness victim.

The Stricken and the Spared

Not everybody exposed to disastrous or deadly events develops PTSD. Even among veterans of battle, which can deliver a barrage of troubling events under conditions of high emotional stimulation, rates of the disorder variety from 10 to 30 percent.

Researchers have been dissecting precisely what makes up strength since the late sociologist Emmy Werner started tracking the development of each baby born upon the island of Kauai in 1955 and discovered that only a minority of those delivered into highly unfavorable circumstances end up struggling or in trouble. For the most part, says psychiatrist Adriana Feder of New York's Mt. Sinai Medical Center, strength research has sought answers in psychosocial elements like family stability and social support, which foster emotional regulation. Only just recently has it deepened to include biology.

Most research into precisely what goes awry in tension circuitry in PTSD looks at people who already have the disorder. However, the most beneficial studies, Feder observes, would look at people before they experience trauma-- like army personnel pre-deployment and people starting work in cops and fire departments-- and follow them.

A pretty big country collective study named AURORA is doing the next best thing. Scientists are gathering data, which includes brain scans, on people seen in emergency rooms instantly after trauma direct exposure and looking for patterns of brain activity that forecast how they fare with time. Feder herself is leading research studies of cops, building workers, and others who reacted to the World Trade Center attacks, comparing the ones that went on to develop PTSD with those that did not.

The 9/11 attacks, terrible as they were, are working as a living lab lighting up the natural course of PTSD. Overall, research studies show, among people exposed to the trauma, PTSD rates declined over the first few years.

Volunteer first responders were significantly more likely to develop PTSD than experts, such as police and firefighters. Volunteers not associated with rescue companies like the Red Cross were especially hard hit, with PTSD rates of nearly 30 percent, vs 13 percent for the pros.

Those data validate earlier findings: Individuals with a history of trauma direct exposure or mental problems and the ones with poor social support and recent or continuous life stress are at high risk of PTSD. An important new finding was that physical impairment or job loss raised the risk of PTSD.

Psychotherapy, including but not limited to exposure treatment utilizing virtual reality, was generally reliable. New data found that children reacted well to psychological therapy provided in school or the community.

IMAGEN is the acronym for a pretty large European study tracking how a wide variety of factors throughout teenage years influences brain development and adult mental health. One of the findings so far is that teenagers who are doing well regardless of the presence of major stressors in their life react in a distinctive way when shown images of afraid or angry faces, normally a stress-inducing circumstance.

Especially, there is little activation of the amygdala. Moreover, research studies show that these youth have more grey matter in the prefrontal cortex. Circuitry associated with cognitive reappraisal-- the ability to reinterpret an event's meaning-- appears associated with more controlled, less excessive reactions.

Can durability be cultivated? Stress-inoculation treatment, usually a component of cognitive behavioral therapy, depends on it. It aims to strengthen people in advance of challenging experiences by exposing them to a development of difficult situations through imagery and video simulations. It seeks to help people develop coping skills; to maintain cognitive flexibility so that troubles can be viewed as challenges to be mastered and chances for development; and to instill a sense of control, the awareness that it's possible to shape the stress reaction by such perceptions. The treatment is often used with people who will be exposed to battle.

It may be that specific drugs given to people instantly before exposure to life-threatening conditions or instantly after can also avert development of PTSD. Among the representatives under study is neuropeptide Y (NPY), a chemical found throughout the nervous system and best understood for promoting food intake.

In the brain, NPY is also associated with resilience to the damaging effects of stress, says neuroscientist Esther Sabban of New York City Medical College. There is some proof that NPY is an all-around inhibitor of nerve action, so it takes a more powerful dose of danger to overactivate stress-circuit nerve cells and dysregulate them. In the amygdala, its release silences the response to stress.

Studies show that people with PTSD have lower blood levels of neuropeptide Y than those who don't develop PTSD. It is unrealistic to know yet whether the distinction precedes their reaction to trauma or is a result of it, although genetic studies suggest it is pre-existing.

In one of her own experiments, performed on rats, Sabban and associates subjected animals to a strong and extended stressor-- the rodent equivalent of trauma. Animals got NPY either thirty minutes before the tension direct exposure, immediately after it, or a week later, when serious stress effects had already set in. NPY given before or instantly after direct exposure to stress entirely blocked development of PTSD-like responses. It had no impact on full-blown symptoms.

Human research studies with NPY are few. One small medical trial found that the neuropeptide given intranasally (to go directly to the brain, averting unwanted impacts on the body) minimized the anxiety symptoms of PTSD. Sabban and her associates are now conducting research that, she hopes, will result in a medical trial big enough to establish whether giving the drug within 2 days after trauma can prevent development of distress to PTSD.

The Reverse of Stress

NPY isn't the only chemical hope against PTSD. Compounds of interest include ketamine, an anesthetic that has a shady past as a club drug called Unique K but which has recently been approved for use to treat extreme, constant sadness, specifically when joined by ideas of suicide. Delivered intravenously, it acts quickly, within hours, although nobody knows exactly how. After years of testing, esketamine (one of 2 nearly similar forms of ketamine) was FDA-approved for resistant sadness early this year.

" A couple of patients we dealt with for depression had PTSD, and their signs appeared to get a lot better too," Adriana Feder reports. "This resulted in our first study, in 2014, with a single intravenous infusion of ketamine." Treatment led to improvement in all symptom groups of PTSD-- re-experiencing the distressing occurrence, avoidance, anhedonia, and hyperarousal-- measured 24 hours later. Feder is now leading a medical trial in which clients get six doses of the drug over a two-week period, "to see whether we can replicate these preliminary findings and maintain the response."

There are strong indicators that ketamine fundamentally alters nerve connection within the brain. "We published a neuroimaging study in depressed patients, which found increased connectivity in emotional control areas after ketamine administration," Feder reports. Her group is now carrying out a similar study in clients with PTSD.

Neuroscientist Ronald Duman, professor of psychiatry and director of molecular psychiatry at Yale University, contends that PTSD is fundamentally a "synaptic deficit disorder"-- blunting communication between individual nerve cells. "A lot of brain imaging work demonstrates reduced volume in brain regions implicated in PTSD. That led to the idea that a loss of synaptic connections could be involved."

A scarcity of connections between afferent neuron would compromise neuroplasticity, hindering learning and keeping those exposed to trauma stuck in their excessive reaction, without any neural escape path-- no pathway for extinguishing the fear response. Animal research has revealed that synapses in the hippocampus and prefrontal cortex dwindle after chronic tension. But proof that the exact same thing happens in PTSD has been elusive. "These are technically very hard studies to do," Duman observes.

There's some indirect evidence of synaptic loss in humans with PTSD. In studies of tissue samples from the PTSD Center's brain bank, scientists have found distinctions in genes regulating synapse formation between individuals with PTSD and those without.

The findings, if validated, could help explain how ketamine works-- both in sadness and PTSD. "Ketamine produces an impact opposite to stress: It increases synaptic connections in the prefrontal cortex, even after a single dose," Duman says.

Synaptic plasticity-- the growth of new inter-neuron connections-- is the foundation of memory and learning. And, in its unraveling, it is the source of the memory-changing procedures that go awry in PTSD.

Normally, the link between a memory and the emotions connected with it can be snuffed out; in time, the emotional reaction element weakens and dissipates. What's more, researchers know that every time a memory is evoked, it can be modified and reframed, a procedure known as reconsolidation. That leads the way for talking about a bad experience with friends in enjoyable surroundings to send the memory back into storage in less disturbing form.

But in PTSD, memories withstand both kinds of change, making them nearly ineradicable. "The memory is always saved in its original form-- they're being raped again, with all of the emotions of the original event," clarifies scientific psychologist Ilan Harpaz-Rotem, also of Yale.

Extended direct exposure and cognitive reappraisal are known to be two of the most effective psychotherapies. They work by advancing memory modification-- the very process paralyzed by PTSD. "Patients need a nudge, and enhanced neurogenesis after ketamine might open a window of reconsolidation," says Harpaz-Rotem.

The Yale researcher is preparing to provide that push, with a clinical trial that integrates ketamine with prolonged exposure therapy. The combination could do in 7 days what, under the best of situations, might otherwise take months. Before-and-after MRI research studies will explore whether and how the treatment changes the way parts of the brain interact.

That's one possibility-- the rapid-acting way. If Ronald Duman is right, there are other ways to restore synaptic connection and mental flexibility. Prime amongst them is exercise, which is known to straight stimulate the growth of new neuronal connections.

" Perhaps a Door"

Paula Scnurr is thrilled about the use of ketamine to "potentiate and enhance the power of the most efficient psychotherapy." It's a circumstances of taking something that works well and making it work even better. Another chemical agent that fits that costs is the psychedelic drug MDMA, aka Ecstasy. "It catalyzes the psychotherapeutic process," says psychiatrist Michael Mithoefer, who has led 20 years of research on MDMA. Extreme interest in its potential has spurred the FDA to designate MDMA a "advancement" treatment for PTSD, and the agency is fast-tracking it towards approval. MDMA is already authorized for use in Israel.

A global Stage III scientific trial-- a huge step to approval-- is already underway. An analysis of six small clinical trials showed that the representative caused sign enhancement

double that of control groups. In the basic protocol, patients are given MDMA before each of three treatment sessions of 8 hours or longer, performed by two specifically trained therapists and spaced a week apart.

" We don't tell people to discuss trauma, but whatever comes up," says Mithoefer. Unstructured as the sessions are, components of standard trauma treatment-- exposure to traumatic material and cognitive restructuring-- are typically engaged. "We stress that MDMA is very different from most psychiatric medications in that it is not developed to quelch signs but to help process underlying causes; at times signs get worse before they get much better."

As a neuroscientist looking into trauma for three decades, psychologist Rachel Yehuda was hesitant of MDMA case reports. "Having actually been in the field for so long and having research experience with many treatments, I could not fathom the claim that after a couple of sessions people with persistent PTSD no longer had it," says Yehuda, director of the Distressing Tension Research Studies

Division at Mt. Sinai Medical Center.

That was before she went to Israel. "I started to understand this was a technique to trauma therapy that involves inducing a really safe and cocooned state for a person." The drug, she says, "produces an open, warm feeling of self-compassion, and the therapist provides an environment for understanding the material that is showing up, making it safe to see from different angles." It removes the barriers where people normally get stuck in psycho-therapy--" where it hurts, the core where they do not want to go."

Yehuda herself underwent a session of treatment, which she says gave her a within comprehension of how the accelerated psychotherapeutic experience cultivates accessing and processing the events of one's life. "It's like learning you can take a plane from New York to Los Angeles, instead of having to walk there."

" Those of us who have tried to comprehend trauma have been searching for a window to help people," Yehuda says. "This may be a floor-to-ceiling window, perhaps a door."

" We know MDMA reduces activity in the amygdala, and increases it in the prefrontal cortex, which fits truly well with what we see clinically: People can unexpectedly speak about their trauma without being gotten rid of by feeling." Mithoefer says. "A veterinarian who went through treatment said, 'Iraq changed my brain, and MDMA changed it back.' There's brain-imaging data to show that."

Regaining Control of Their Own Brains

All the imaging studies checking out the neurobiology of PTSD have helped determine "which brain areas need to be turned up and which denied," says Paul Holtzheimer, deputy director for research at the National Center for PTSD. And that opens the way for highly targeted treatments, including neurofeedback.

" When you fear something, the amygdala ends up being triggered; in PTSD it is triggered more," says Ilan Harpaz-Rotem. With neurofeedback, patients learn how to minimize signs by calling back brain activity by themselves. Particularly after being at the mercy of unforeseeable triggers anytime and anywhere, "it's empowering for them to take control of their own brains," he says.

Harpaz-Rotem is leading a clinical trial in which individuals with PTSD lie in an MRI scanner, watching a guideline that tracks blood flow-- an indication of amygdala activity-- while they are read a script and hear noises evocative of the speeding up trauma. They are taught techniques to lower fear and, by watching the guideline, can figure out which ones moisten amygdala stimulation.

The hope is that they will use the strategies whenever they feel overwhelmed, "not to eliminate the memories but to learn to tolerate them," he says. Before-and-after MRIs will reveal any transformed connection between the amygdala, the hippocampus, and the prefrontal cortex and any connections with sign reduction.

Another promising treatment takes direct focus on the malfunctioning circuitry of PTSD and gives it a reboot. Transcranial magnetic stimulation, which applies a shifting electromagnetic field to produce small electric currents in pertinent areas, is already in usage for drug-resistant depression and obsessive-compulsive disorder.

In PTSD, it targets an essential neural node-- the dorsolateral prefrontal cortex. The objective is to boost cognitive control so the brain can better regulate feeling, decreasing the intensity of undesirable experiences. "The effects might rollover to certain symptoms-- avoidance, even flashbacks," says Holtzheimer.

Brain stimulation is being tested as a psychotherapy booster, too. Applied just prior to weekly sessions of cognitive reprocessing therapy, the treatment,

Holtzheimer worries, is still very much an operate in progress. "If it follows the same timeline as that for sadness, perhaps in 5 years we will see a pivotal scientific trial that opens the door to broad availability."

The capability to treat PTSD efficiently is advancing in lockstep with new comprehension of the disorder. Horrible events will continue to happen; even if war were to stop tomorrow, nature provides its own random blows. Emotional aftershocks will inevitably resound in the minds and brains of those exposed. However, while pain is inescapable, enduring suffering is not. Putting an end to it is no longer a difficult goal.

Chapter 8: Appointment Preparation

Before seeking treatment, you will need information on what to prepare for your appointment. Going to an appointment fully prepared provides you with a link to all the information you will need to gain the full potential out of every visit. At appointments, you need to gain all the information you need and want to know to gain a full understanding of the process.

What to Prepare:

Your medical information such as records and medical history. Your doctor will always request for this in order to see whether you have any previous mental or physical illnesses that may contribute to the onset or worsening of PTSD. A further, in depth psychological history or any psych tests (if available) would also help your doctor in measuring the scope of the traumas effects on you.

It would help to make a list of your personal information, unofficial things that often aren't included in medical records such as experiences you have recently had, any recent trips you took, anything you may have seen. Make this list days before your appointment in order to allow yourself leeway to add to it should you remember anything significant.

Make a list of the symptoms you may be feeling such as not wanting to leave the house, not wanting to talk to people or socialize. Also, things that you now view as threatening or scary such as toy guns, watching TV, swimming pools. Everything you have experienced that has, recently, become out of the ordinary as compared to otherwise.

It would also help if you seek for the assistance of a family member or a close friend. Not only will you be provided with support but they can also aid you in remembering situations that you have been through recently as well as point out a few symptoms that they have observed that you may have missed in your list.

What information should I get from my doctor?

After speaking to your doctor, ask him what his opinion is on the source of the symptoms.

Know whether there are any other possible causes that might be making the symptoms occur. Being absolutely sure that it is PTSD and not anything else is important in determining the next course of treatment.

Find out about diagnosis methods and how this will be determined.

Know what all the treatment options are as well as your doctor's top recommendation. Having choices is a good thing, but having a professional medical recommendation behind a choice is even better.

If you have other underlying health problems besides PTSD, ask your doctor about how you can deal with them and whether maintenance medication (if any) might affect your treatment.

Find out how long you will be in treatment before you start to feel significant changes in yourself and in your outlook on life.

Query whether PTSD might be the root cause for the occurrence of other health or mental problems.

Ask your doctor what changes you can make (to your capabilities) that could help the treatment process; this might include changes in work, or at home.

Would recovery be affected in any possible positive or negative way if work colleagues, bosses, or teachers were informed of the disorder?

Improving your knowledge on PTSD is always one sure way to gain a full understanding of your disorder which will enable you towards a better and quicker treatment process. Ask your doctor about any additional sources of information that can tell you more about PTSD. But if you are reading this, you've already got it.

Your doctor is there for you to aid you in the healing process and he understands that the more information you have and alternatively, the less questions you will have, the more you will understand the occurrence of PTSD and hence its treatment process. Do not hesitate to ask your doctor anything you need or want to know.

What your doctor will want to know:

This is a complied list of the most common things that patients with PTSD are asked by their doctors. You can read and prepare for these questions in advance, that way you don't miss out on any pieces of vital information.

Your doctor will want to know what your symptoms are. As mentioned above make a list of your symptoms days in advance in order to give yourself extra time to list down more things that you may have missed.

You will also be asked when you first began to feel the symptoms that you have listed down. For a more in depth estimation, ask a family member when they began to notice the symptoms as well.

The event that may have caused your trauma. Your doctor will need specifics such as when, where, how, and who was involved. Do not feel overwhelmed or pressured, you do not have to share this information all at once, tell the doctor what you can or have a family member present to tell him for you.

How do you feel physically and emotionally? Do you feel like you have been abused, or have you been sexually assaulted.

Whether or not you are experiencing uncontrollable thoughts that occur at random times and cannot be controlled or stopped. Relating to this are also nightmares or day dreams.

Whether you have experiences of lucidity, like you aren't dreaming of these traumatic experiences re-occurring.

Whether there are certain places, people, or situations that you avoid in order to lessen the anxiety felt by the feelings they bring on.

The activities and hobbies that you used to enjoy that you have now greatly and suddenly lost interest in.

Whether or not you feel easily irritated and angry even for reasons you know are irrational.

Do you find it difficult to fall asleep? Are you restless during the night? Sleep late and wake up early?

Current occurrences or presences in your life that may be giving you a feeling of danger or that are making you anxious. Such as a swimming pool in the backyard if you have just been through a life threatening situation of drowning while on vacation at the seaside.

The state of your relationships with family, friends, and work colleagues. Also, whether they are the same as what they used to be or if contact has become substantially decreased.

Have you ever experienced thoughts of self-harm or purposely causing harm to others?

Whether or not you engage in substance abuse or take in alcohol. If the answer to this is yes, you r doctor will want to know the quantity and frequency.

Whether or not you have had past bouts of mental instability either for this same reason or for something else.

Chapter 9: Emotional And Physical Trauma – Methods Of Overcoming Them

Emotional trauma can be just as fragile as physical trauma. The unintended side effect of physical trauma is emotional trauma. Whilst emotional trauma without physical trauma may occur, emotional trauma physically affects us. The trauma's weakening effects are well known. Therefore, it is important to recover from any trauma if a person wants to live a life as safe as possible.

Security is the most important ingredient in recovery from any trauma. It must ensure that safe people are a must in safe places. The best are those trained to listen, be unjustified, and feel empathic. My understanding is that most of these individuals are psychologists and mental counselors. Continuing work supports thinking about a trauma experience with another person as the best way to recover from trauma. Tell the story as many times as necessary to extract from you the burden of full responsibility, try to make sense of the trauma, and incorporate the experience into our own understanding. The traumatic experience can also be experienced at different levels, including at the somatic and visual levels.

Having a therapist/counselor with whom you feel safe is a challenge — some posts on finding a good therapist and what good therapy is written. A good therapist doesn't make a person dysfunctional but perceives a client as greater than his / her issues. A good therapist also understands that a person must manage his / her issues if he/she shows frustration and learn to cope with and express that anger safely. A good therapist won't call a client a "fearful person." Great therapists also know how to inspire their clients, and many people have changed and become healthier. A good therapist knows his own skills, is sensitive, caring, imaginative, and reliable.

There is a spirit of cooperation in good therapy, and the interaction between the therapist and the client is important. Good therapy is both verbal and cognitive, using emotional and cognitive strategies that allow a person to heal emotionally and holistically. A good therapist can also refer a client to another therapist if it is the customer's best judgment.

Working in a group is another powerful way to heal traumatic experiences. At a party, a consumer may find out that many people have similar problems. The benefit is to listen to various Strategies that benefited various people. Although helping organizations are excellent for this form of treatment, therapeutic groups can be better. A support group consists of people with similar problems and often has no qualified leader. A counseling group is also composed of people with similar problems, but the group phase is guided by a trained therapist. Training is an important part of trauma rehabilitation.

Therapists have been trained and often use research-based methods, such as Dialectic Behavioral Therapy, to promote group work.

Sometimes a person works on a trauma they are conscious of, and underneath it has reminders of other trauma. Sometimes our unresolved unconscious memories of our early childhood contribute to similar situations being recreated in an attempt to solve early childhood trauma. Our implicit memory is hard to create a "self-accomplishing prophecy." As a person is working on a current trauma, he or she will also focus on previous trauma.

It is important for people to examine the type of therapy that they want to use. The use of expressive therapies is supported recently by research. Expressive therapies include the recognition and validation of trauma emotions. Emotions involve a number of processes that are essential for the mind. Cognitions and feelings work together. They work together. They can't be separated. Emotions connect with people. Unfortunately, in the first three years of their lives, many people did not experience a healthy relationship, which often leads to people unable to be aware of their feelings. It is important to be aware of our feelings; they also provide us with important information. Trauma may cause people to anesthetize their feelings. Such attempts often take the form of addiction. Many times a person simply sees himself as having no feelings or as being "not emotional." Expressive therapy can be extremely helpful for both these individuals and for those who are more mindful of their feelings.

A cognitive and verbal mix of interventions is often the best. Expressive therapy can produce relatively easy emotions. Cognitive therapy can be used to teach cognitive coping skills. Conduct is a product of thoughts and feelings. Competencies should improve as the emotional and cognitive health of the person improves. A trait of good therapy is the therapist's ability to meet a client, "where he is." The extremely intellectualized client would be an example of this. A good therapist begins with a lot of educational and cognitive training as he incorporates emotional and verbal work.

Spiritual Energy, Trauma and The Body Mind

Many, if not most of us, have been affected in some form by trauma. Any event or series of events, real or imagined, which triggers the body's mentally bad distress and which the person sees is unable to avoid or track, can be traumatic. The consequences of a single trauma or sequence of traumas and their recovery depend on many factors, including karma, both for the soul and the body.

Although historically, we consider trauma like physical or serious traumatic events such as wars or disasters, the psychological community has recognized that frequent declines or other unsuitable encounters can have a profound effect on the psyche. The values we have learned from our families also serve as a model of affection for our future relationships. Medical problems and increasingly invasive methods will easily add to life's trauma reservoir. The social stress and peer pressure, particularly in the sexual arena, all contribute to the warehouse in which we live.

We have two conflicting karmic tracks: the soul that lives in one lifespan and has many incarnations, and the body that has a genetic history across successive generations. We each bear the implicit burden of trauma, remorse, and patterns of attraction. When tandem with the present traumatic experience, this can be an unbearable responsibility. The soul's karma is psychologically contained in consciousness, which influences the physicality of that manifestation, where and when we are embodied. The body is energized into the multiple layers of the body-mind, which then can affect consciousness.

We have different acupuncture meridians that are more fragile than others, depending on our genetic heritage. The method of acupuncture is in the esthetic or esthetic body. When there is an energetic/emotional impact on the body's mind, the meridian(s) are affected and begin to decline at some point, which can result in pain in their respective organs or system.

Some of those with memories of sexual abuse seem to have embraced the fantasies and guilty ideas of the adults they were exposed to. Children are very responsive mentally, so reading the minds of those around them is not unusual. Perhaps people with obsessive compulsive behaviors are trying to protect themselves from other people's intrusive thinking. It doesn't matter to the human consciousness if it was a real event or if it is taken from another, but it is nevertheless real.

Patterns of dysfunction can be genetically inherited for many generations. Disable energetic encoding, and the pattern can be broken more quickly. Moms traumatized themselves also hold the energy in their solar plexus, which can imprint on the fetus. Sperm can also bear the father's energetic as well as genetic residue at conception. If trauma is unsolved, this imprint can be inserted into the sperm that leads to the offspring. Obviously, there is the whole cycle of parental suffering in which to succeed.

For many people, particularly those whose suffering was due to human actions, guilt and shame also add up to the strain. Sexually abused children or young adults often have the embarrassment of the positive reaction of the body to the violence as well as shame that arises from different misunderstandings. The perpetrators of tragic events like the Holocaust are guilty of any perceived misdeeds committed both for survival and the simple fact of having survived.

Naturally, every person will respond to a certain stimulus differently, and that which is slumped by one can become a deep wound in another. After a lightning strike, what makes one tree prosper and another falter and die? The factors involved are more than the stars that are visible in the sky, and nobody can really predict the result.

The list of symptoms shown by people due to trauma is quite different. They are responsible for the range of human dysfunction, including the original wound. In many situations, an energy boost is analogous to an electric condenser that releases an extreme pressure to overcome inertia. Whenever the trigger is triggered, an overwhelming energy release threatens to consume the human. This can turn the treatment into a potentially volatile task.

Psychologists and spiritual / energy healers have taken tremendous strides in several decades to recognize and to establish effective tools for coping with trauma. Various modes use sensor switches, such as quick eye motion and taping to disperse trigger mechanisms. Some are actively working on letting the energy run out while others are seeking to disseminate the Karmic debt, reducing the level of conscious culpability dramatically. Soul healing is being used in many situations to put together the broken portions of the individual, and the growing popularity of 12-step programs has helped others escape the misery of drug abuse, promoting exposure to underlying diseases.

Regardless of the specific course of action or variations that arise following trauma, rehabilitation involves courage and determination by the customer/patient and a strong commitment to healing. It also needs the therapist to have a high level of expertise and experience. In any case, the growing recognition of these problems and increasingly successful coping strategies offer hope for those who have historically been stuck in their past experiences.

Trauma and PTSD - Post Traumatic Stress Disorder Treatment With Hypnotherapy

Trauma is something most of us will have to deal with on our life journey at some point. Yes, it is projected that sometimes 50% to 90% of us will have to deal with it.

Psychological trauma is always a product of an experience that overwhelms the victim and does not handle or fully control the emotions produced by that experience.

The subconscious mind is disturbed by distress by an incident or a number of events, and this has profoundly affected the individual's functioning.

Essential and effective though it is certainly for the traumatized individual, the actual experience itself is less essential on a psychological level than its interpretation and reaction.

It explains why one person can very well shrug a similar event off but creates real difficulties in another. What can be a traumatic experience is not traumatic for one person.

Trauma itself can happen on a life journey at any time.

This can occur during infancy, and as a result of, for example, psychological, physical abuse, or extreme poverty and can leave the child traumatized in adulthood.

And traumas arise later in life, triggered by neglect, injuries, injury, crime, war, death, and natural disaster.

Although trauma itself is painful, about 8% are more debilitating and paralyzing effects of the Post Traumatic Stress Disorder (PTSD) trauma.

If left untreated, PTSD can have serious consequences for the patient, serious implications, and ability to function at work or interpersonal level.

PTSD also stems from real physical damage encounters or experiences. Occasionally, however, psychological and emotional distress may cause it where no actual physical harm is involved.

Very often, though, it blends both aspects.

While a persistent and significant emotional response to trauma is essentially post-traumatic stress disorder, it differs from combat stress or traumatic stress in that it is typically much more severe and not at all transitory.

PTSD has also historically been identified as shell shock, combat tiredness, and post-traumatic stress syndrome.

Yet fighting is not sufficient to be affected by PTSD, any real trauma to the nervous system—such as a car accident or death, addiction to drugs or sexual assault—can lead to it.

However, whatever the cause, the resulting symptoms of trauma are real and distressing for a person who has to experience them.

Those with this type of trauma can experience chronic and acute anxiety, frustration, sleep disturbance, disturbing thoughts, breathtaking disorder, or nightmares. We also find it very difficult to think about trauma cases.

We find it difficult or impossible to effectively deal with and incorporate these issues on the subconscious level of the mind, owing to their upsetting nature.

And here, transformational hypnotherapy with experience can be extremely useful, offering psychological care that can lead to a full recovery from trauma.

The unconscious mind, working with a skilled and highly trained transformational hypnotherapist, can be guided to reconstitute traumatic experiences of the past in order to neutralize and reverse the damage.

The truth is that the person survived, given the frightening expectations and beliefs that were instilled during the traumatic experience. Ultimately, he or she did it through.

Chapter 10: Mind Body Synergy

Simply put, the brain remembers, the body remembers, no matter how much you consciously remember or wish you could forget, the brain remembers and the body remembers. Post-Traumatic Stress is seated in pain and pain is intoxicating. It is common for folks to avoid pain, ignore pain, many people just wait and hope it passes, sometimes it does, sometimes it doesn't, but the resounding fact of PTS is that the pain does not pass on its own; in fact, it creates more pain as the brain has been rewired by this unanswerable unending question to our safety. It intrudes in our lives, defending aggressively against mixed signals, or reliving horrors in great detail.

Research is discovering the destructive aspects of PTSD on the brain, physical wellbeing, and emotional health of survivors. The brain actually shrinks when bathed in the intoxicants of pain over and over again during the onslaught of PTSD symptoms; however the brain also grows as we counteract and combat these harmful effects. The brain is a beautiful experience, when certain areas are lost or disconnected, other areas can counteract. Through diligent healing practices you can become reconnected with yourself, grounded with yourself, have unobstructed lives again, and literally, rewire your brain.

In Western Medicine, the approach has largely been based in medication assisted talk-therapy, a costly approach with many limitations considering that PTS is largely stored in the body and inaccessible to regions of the brain where trauma is stored. It is not necessarily relieved through talking or re-experiencing, medication can assist, however this also is limited in its abilities to tap into the brain's ability to heal itself with effort and the right conditions.

If you are a living with PTS, the experience is over, yet alive and well inside of you; healing is inside of you as well. The body and mind act in synergy and when PTS symptoms arise there is an impact within, whether it is an escalated heart rate, churning stomach, or a feeling of sickness, the body knows and is responding to the alarms. It is essential to become familiar with your process. The journey from trigger, to internal response, to external reaction, to result is all essential to understanding and dismantling the destructive process of PTS. On the other hand, if you feel more like a ticking time bomb and don't know these triggers but feel sick or anxious or explosive all the time, that's also ok, these techniques will also relieve those unknown energies. There are methods in this book that do not require any thought, belief, or remembering, they work directly with the physical storage of trauma and can be substantial in progressing with PTS without reliving or re-experiencing, most notably of these techniques is Trauma Releasing Exercises and **EFT**.

Symptoms

The symptoms of PTS share many things in common with other mental health diagnoses, except with PTS, the symptoms are attached to the experience of a traumatic event. I would argue that the majority of mental health concerns are connected to the experience of trauma, but that is another book entirely. For our purposes, as PTS survivors, our symptoms indicate that we are not yet healed. No matter how long a trauma is buried, regardless of how long we have 'worked' towards recovery, if we are experiencing symptoms of PTS we are not YET healed.

Symptoms while they can often be frustrating, embarrassing, alienating, and sometimes humiliating, for our purposes and from this point forward, our symptoms only indicate to us that we are not yet healed, nothing more and nothing less. It is common to over-identify with symptoms as if I am my symptoms and others also feed this false thinking with statements like "he's an angry person," "she's an anxious person."

For anyone seeking to free themselves from PTS it is important to understand that we are not our symptoms. On a path of recovery, our symptoms are only a roadmap to the healing we need to achieve. Every outburst or breakdown holds the keys to healing, has all the ingredients of recovery, and everyone can be used to further our own healing and become a stronger and more resilient human being.

In this text, we do not visit symptoms in detail as each person while similar has a unique experience and understanding. I encourage you to explore identifying your symptoms of discomfort, escalations, outbursts, or numbness. Be creative, give them your own names and become familiar with them. For more information on this process visit the Resources section of our **website**.

Re-experiencing

Re-experiencing is exactly that, it is fresh and in color, intrusively, repeatedly, in the shower, in bed, in the middle of the night, our traumatic history invades our minds and emotions. Our body responds and we feel the emotions attached to the event that we may not have even felt at the time, but we feel it now; the terror, the disgust, the fear, the helplessness and hopelessness. In that moment we are victimized again, and it can become increasingly worse as we struggle with all the aftershocks of a traumatic event, re-experiencing can almost haunt us as we struggle to recover a sense of self and power again.

The natural and instinctual coping response to re-experiencing is avoidance, when a message, a sound, a word, a touch, a tone of voice or an environment triggers re-experiencing it may be best to avoid those triggers. However this is not always possible, especially if these triggers are attached to necessary activities of living, like working, grocery shopping, going to a doctor's appointment, or other healthy and life affirming activities. Similarly, in a traumatic experience surrounding a current abusive relationship, it is not always possible to avoid the triggering person or environment at all.

Avoidance may currently be the best coping skill at your disposal and with time and increased practice with the skills described in this book, there may become less of a need to react with avoidance. Furthermore, as the harm of re-experiencing isn't necessarily the re-experience itself but the cascade of symptoms it precipitates, I encourage you to begin to watch and identify the journey from trigger, to response, to reaction to begin to apply successful coping strategies to symptoms before and after they occur.

Coping Skill

☐ Identify Reaction to Re-Experiencing and Complete Coping Exercise for Symptom

☐ Avoidance

☐ Dissociation

☐ Intrusive Thoughts

☐ Hypervigilance

☐ Anxiety

☐ Depression

☐ Depersonalization/Derealization

Conclusion

Hopefully by now you have some brain hacks and healing techniques in your arsenal to use to help aid you in the healing process. You should have a better understanding of how to deal with CPTSD, PTSD, and take back control of your life. Remember that this world is not friendly to those of us with mental disorders and it can affect the rest of your life if you are not careful. Do not lose your rights because you though your PTSD was a "get out of jail free" card; it does not work that way.

Empower yourself through self-defense classes and feel like you can defend yourself through discipline and a sense of security. You should find some comfort in knowing you will not be a push-over and have some ways to protect yourself. Find some time for yourself and try some anxiety relief by trying some EFT tapping or a massage to rid yourself of past trauma's.

I know it can feel like you may get triggered and cannot help it but try to understand what and why you do get "set-off" and become reactive. Understanding and being aware of what is happening to you is half the battle. Start fresh and try to reprogram your thought patterns through subconscious mind. We operate on 5% of our conscious throughout the day and 95 % on our pre-programmed subconscious. If you can utilize some brain hacks like positive affirmations, changing negative thoughts into neutral thoughts, using the "mindbus" technique, changing your perception of yourself, being grateful, or even just working on your smile can help change your attitude and outlook on life.

Do not underestimate a good diet filled with dopamine and serotonin-rich foods to help fight against depression and keep your mind and body healthy. Exercise and the right combinations of food will help keep you mentally alert and make sure to get your full night sleep away from artificial sunlight. There are many brain hacks and ways to help you deal with your CPTSD and PTSD. So, give yourself what you deserve and get on track to becoming a better you and remember it is all mind over matter.

www.ingramcontent.com/pod-product-compliance
Lightning Source LLC
LaVergne TN
LVHW011952070526
838202LV00054B/4909